Suzanne Francis

lives in Los Angeles with her husband, their two children and a curly-tailed beast. In addition to writing, Suzanne can play the piano, swim and eat kale.

Dominic Carola

is an award-winning animator, artist and creative director working in the animation, publishing, theme park and film industries. As an alumnus of CalArts and a veteran of Walt Disney Feature Animation, he currently serves as an independent producer and director of Premise Entertainment. Learn more about Dominic at PremiseEntertainment.com.

Ryan Feltman

is a veteran artist who has enjoyed illustrating children's books and doing visual development, concept and animation work for the past ten years. He enjoys life in Florida with his wife and their three beautiful children.

A Friend Like Him

Written by Suzanne Francis
Illustrated by Dominic Carola and Ryan Feltman

SCHOLASTIC
SYDNEY AUCKLAND NEW YORK TORONTO LONDON MEXICO CITY
NEW DELHI HONG KONG BUENOS AIRES PUERTO RICO

For Jack

—S. F.

To good friends that I've been honoured
to work and share life with

—D. C.

To my loving wife for all her support,
allowing me to live my dream
as a professional artist

—R. F.

Copyright © 2019 Disney Enterprises, Inc. All rights reserved.
Published by Scholastic Australia in 2019.
Scholastic Australia Pty Limited
PO Box 579 Gosford NSW 2250
ABN 11 000 614 577
www.scholastic.com.au
Part of the Scholastic Group
Sydney • Auckland • New York • Toronto • London • Mexico City
New Delhi • Hong Kong • Buenos Aires • Puerto Rico
All rights reserved. No part of this publication may be reproduced or transmitted in any form or by any means, electronic or mechanical, including photocopying, recording, storage in an information retrieval system, or otherwise, without the prior written permission of the publisher, unless specifically permitted under the Australian Copyright Act 1968 as amended.
ISBN 978-1-76066-584-5
Printed in China by RR Donnelley.
Scholastic Australia's policy, in association with RR Donnelley, is to use papers that are renewable and made efficiently from wood grown in responsibly managed forests, so as to minimise its environmental footprint.
10 9 8 7 6 5 4 3 2 1   19 20 21 22 23 / 1

This is the genie.

Everyone calls him . . .

GENIE.

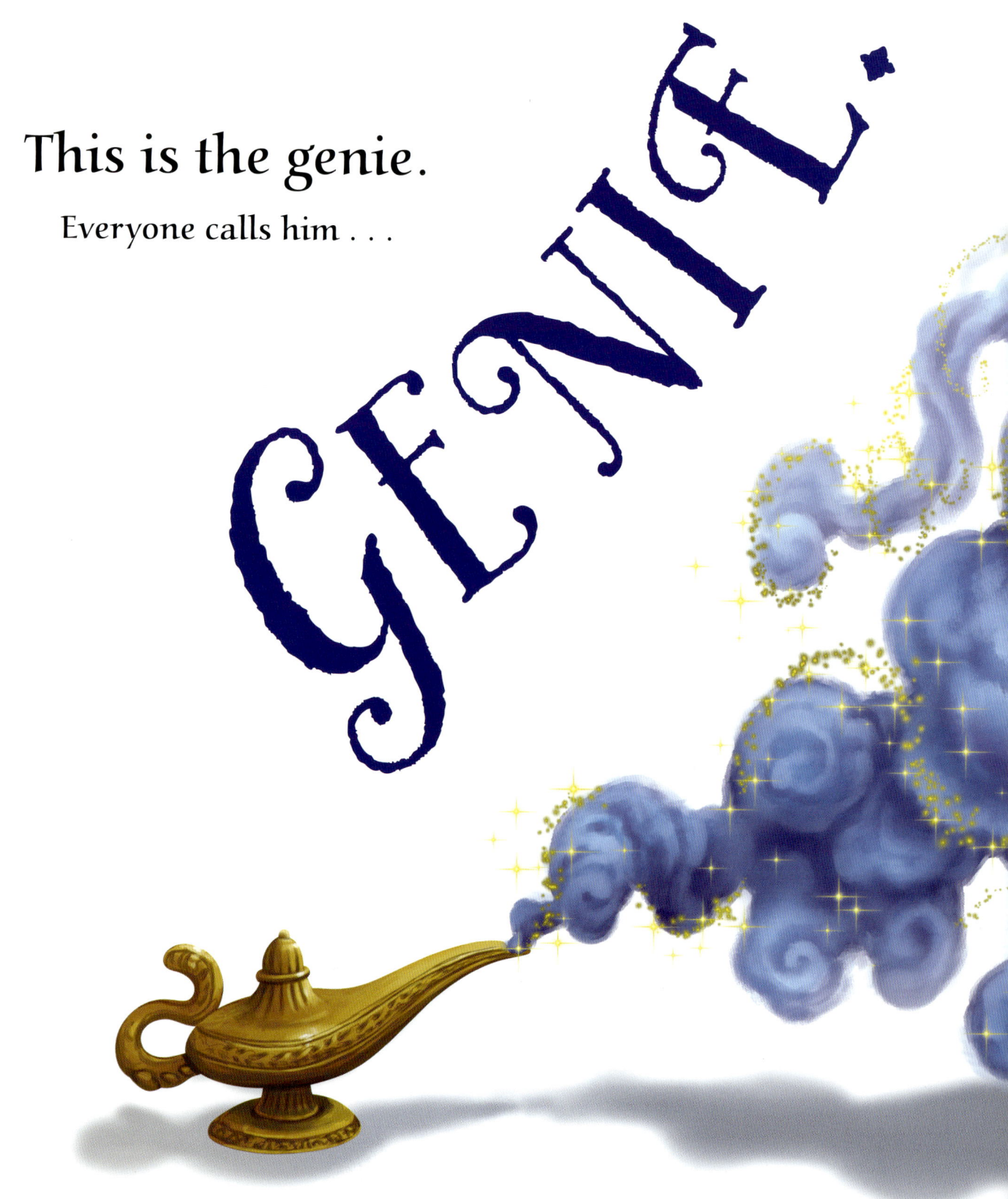

He spends LOADS of time inside his teeny-tiny home,
which happens to be a lamp.

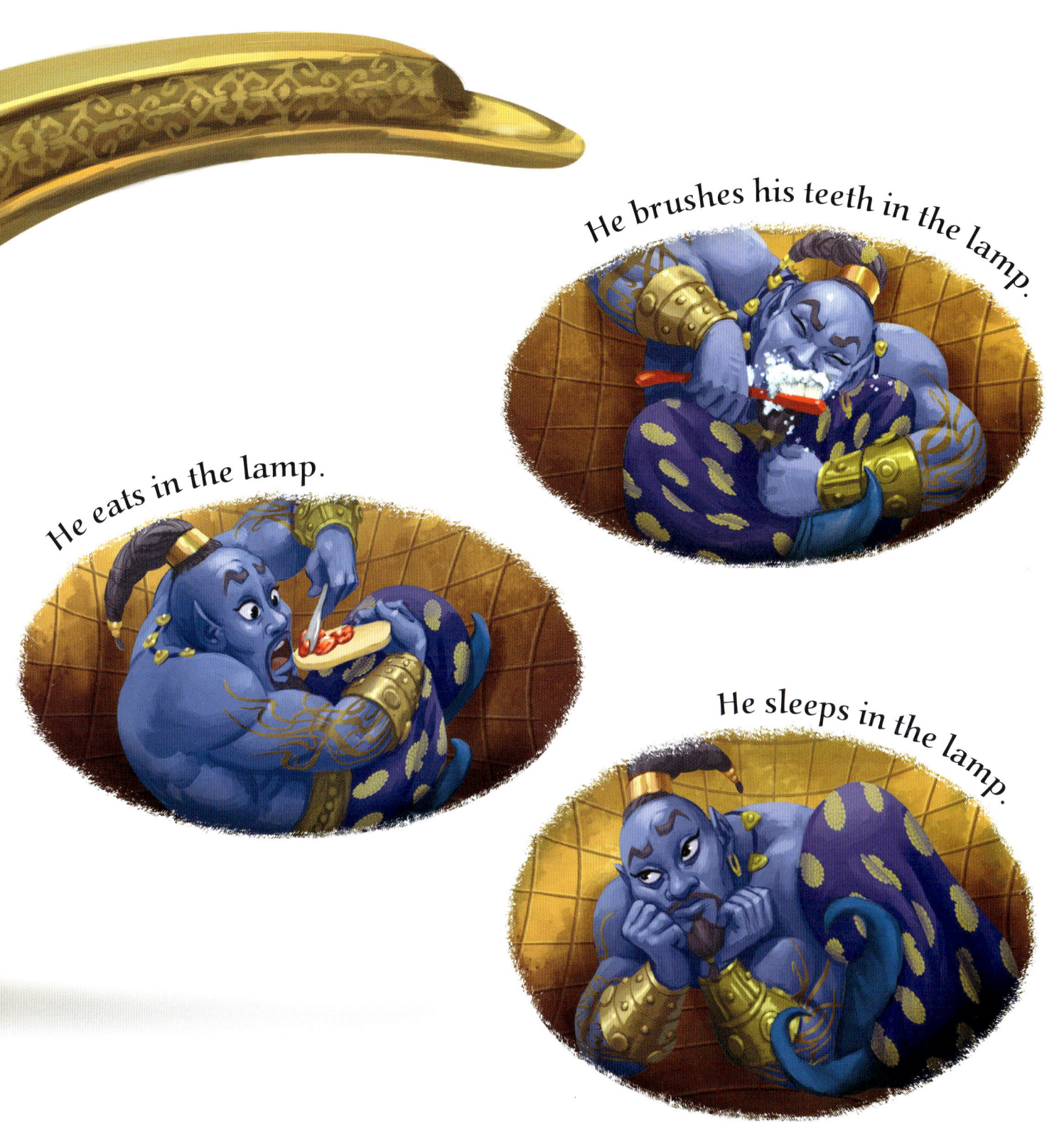

He brushes his teeth in the lamp.

He eats in the lamp.

He sleeps in the lamp.

But more than anything else, he stares at lots and lots of brass. It gets pretty boring and lonely.

Genie only comes OUT of the lamp if somebody finds it.
And that is quite a task, because it's usually buried in some deep,
dark, scary place ... like a magical cave in the middle of the desert.

When somebody does find the lamp, they rub it and . . .

WHOOSH!

Out comes Genie.

Then they can ask for THREE WISHES.
Genie uses his magic to grant each one.

Lots of the people who find Genie's lamp have a certain look in their eyes. They know exactly what they want . . . and it's usually money, power or fame.

LIKE THIS GUY.

AND THIS GUY.

Every few hundred years or so,
there is someone who finds the lamp accidentally.

LIKE THIS CAMEL.

AND THIS BABY.

But one day a very different kind of person found Genie's lamp. His name was ALADDIN. He went into the deep, dark, dangerous magical cave because a man—much like the others—had tricked him.

Aladdin didn't know anything about Genie or his magic.
But when he rubbed some dirt off the side of the lamp . . .

WHOOSH!

Something magical happened.

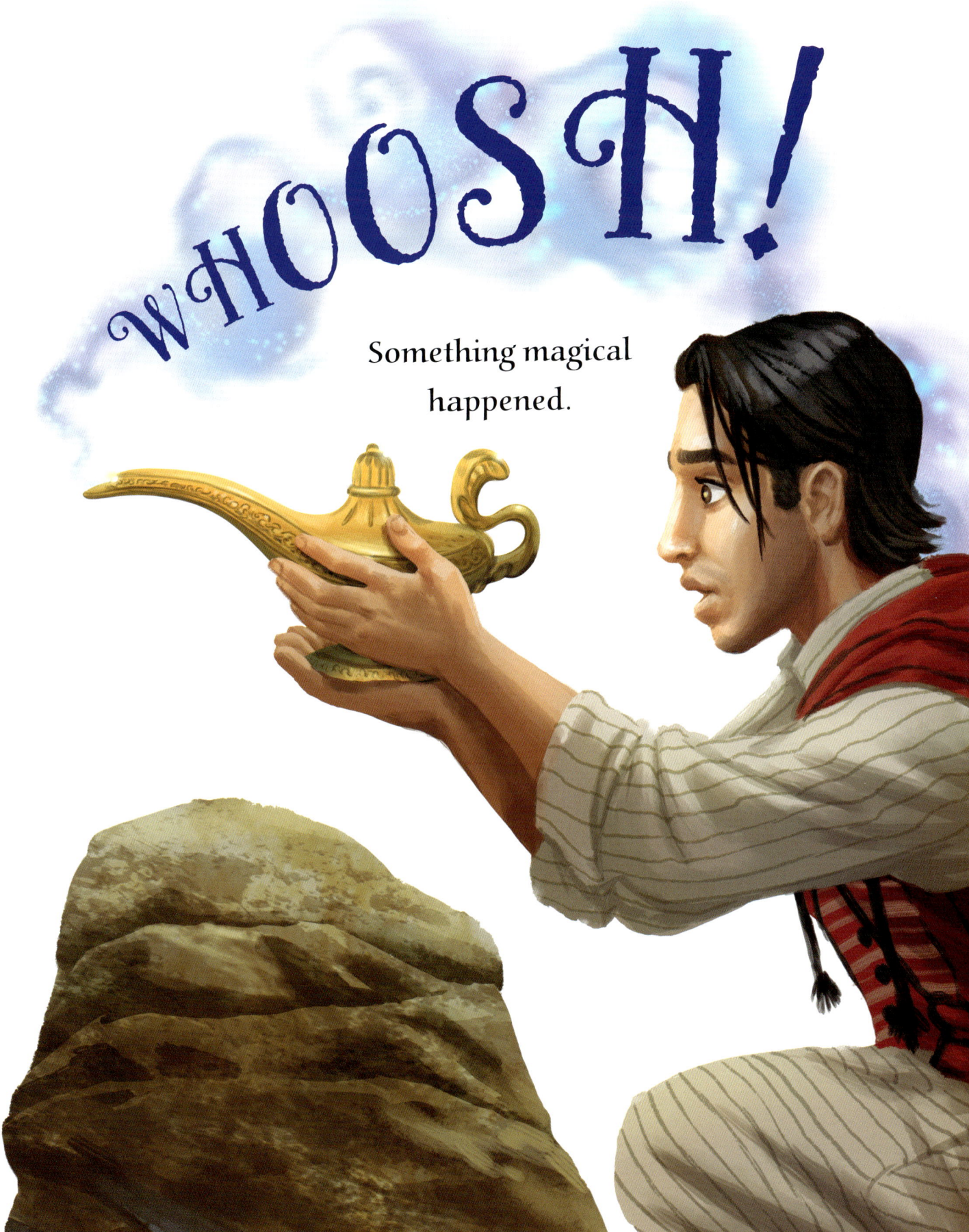

Genie emerged.
Aladdin had never seen anything like that before.
He thought Genie was a giant. He had never even heard of genies!

Genie could tell right away that Aladdin was different. He didn't have that creepy look in his eyes, and he asked how long Genie had been inside the lamp. Genie was happy to answer:

"BOUT A THOUSAND YEARS."

Aladdin was amazed . . . and still very confused.

Genie was more than happy to demonstrate his incredible skills.

Aladdin couldn't believe all that Genie could do. But he still didn't understand how the whole thing worked.

Genie explained. 'You have three wishes, and they must begin with rubbing the lamp and saying: "I WISH." GOT IT?'

Aladdin nodded. Then Genie pointed out some basic rules.

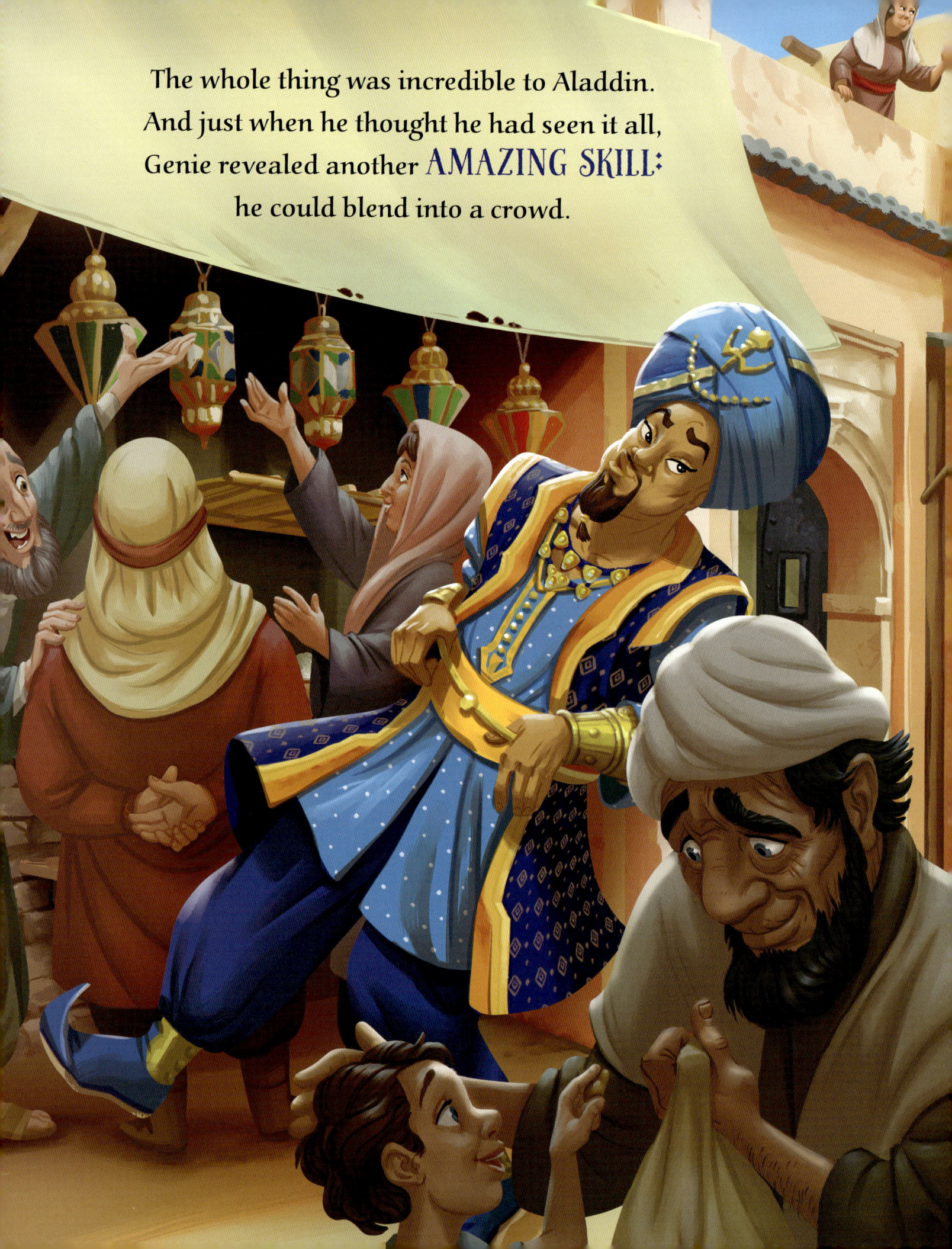

The whole thing was incredible to Aladdin. And just when he thought he had seen it all, Genie revealed another AMAZING SKILL: he could blend into a crowd.

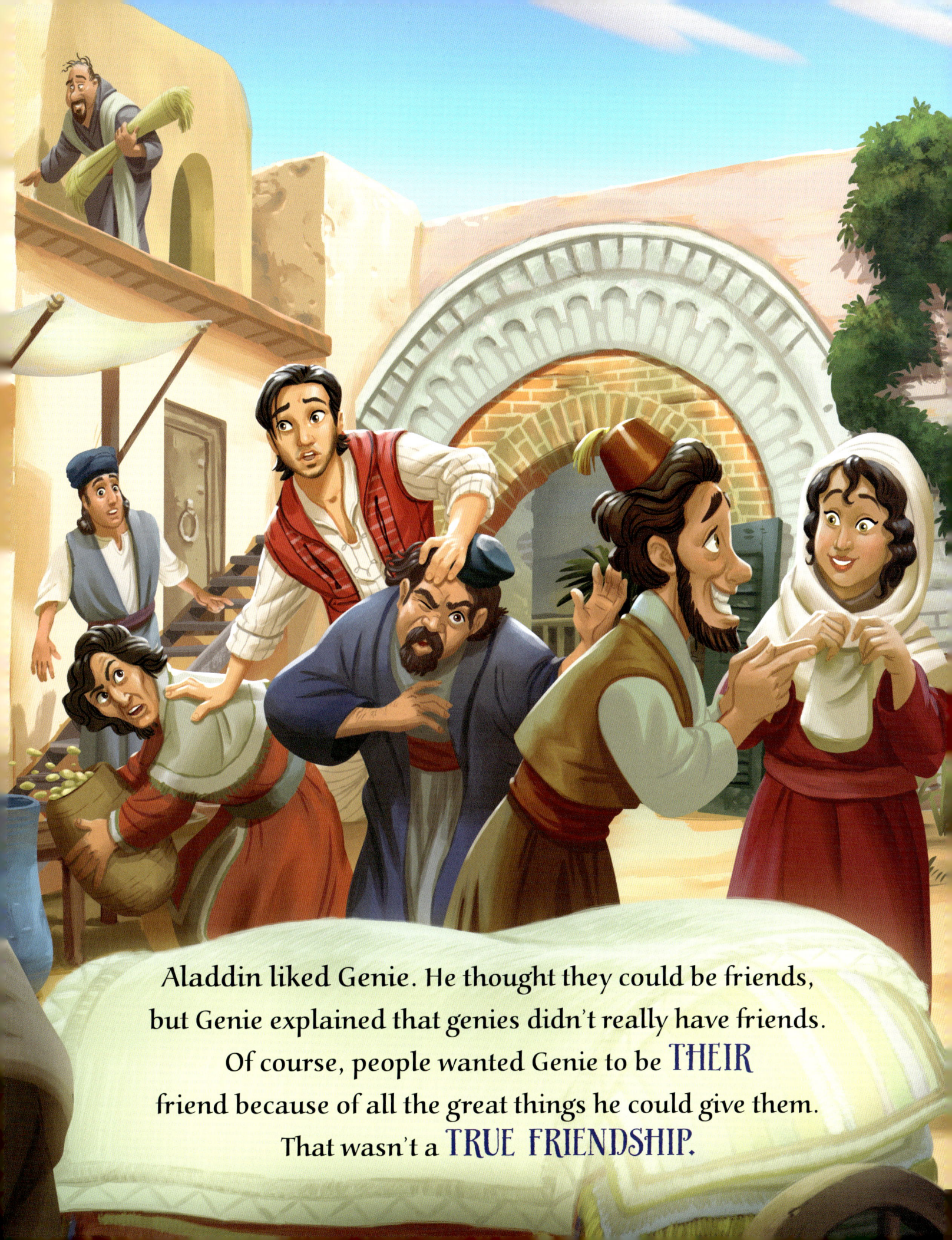

Aladdin liked Genie. He thought they could be friends, but Genie explained that genies didn't really have friends. Of course, people wanted Genie to be THEIR friend because of all the great things he could give them. That wasn't a TRUE FRIENDSHIP.

But Genie kind of liked Aladdin, so he also told him
how important it was to correctly word a wish.
'Use your words—avoid sticky misunderstandings,' he said.

He explained how one guy's wish to be
'MOST ATTRACTIVE'
turned him into a human magnet.

Another's wish to be
'RICH AND HANDSOME'
landed him a new name.

And when someone else said,
'MAKE ME A PRINCE,'
he ended up with a little royal
dude following him around.

When Aladdin asked Genie what he would wish for, Genie was stunned. 'Wow . . . nobody's ever asked me that before. But that's easy.' Genie's wish was to live outside the lamp and never have to grant another wish again!

Aladdin wanted to impress Princess Jasmine.
After giving it some thought, he said,

'I WISH TO BECOME A PRINCE.'

Hearing Aladdin's perfectly worded wish, Genie nodded proudly. He could tell Aladdin had been listening.

With some big Genie magic . . .

BOOM!

Aladdin became Prince Ali of Ababwa.

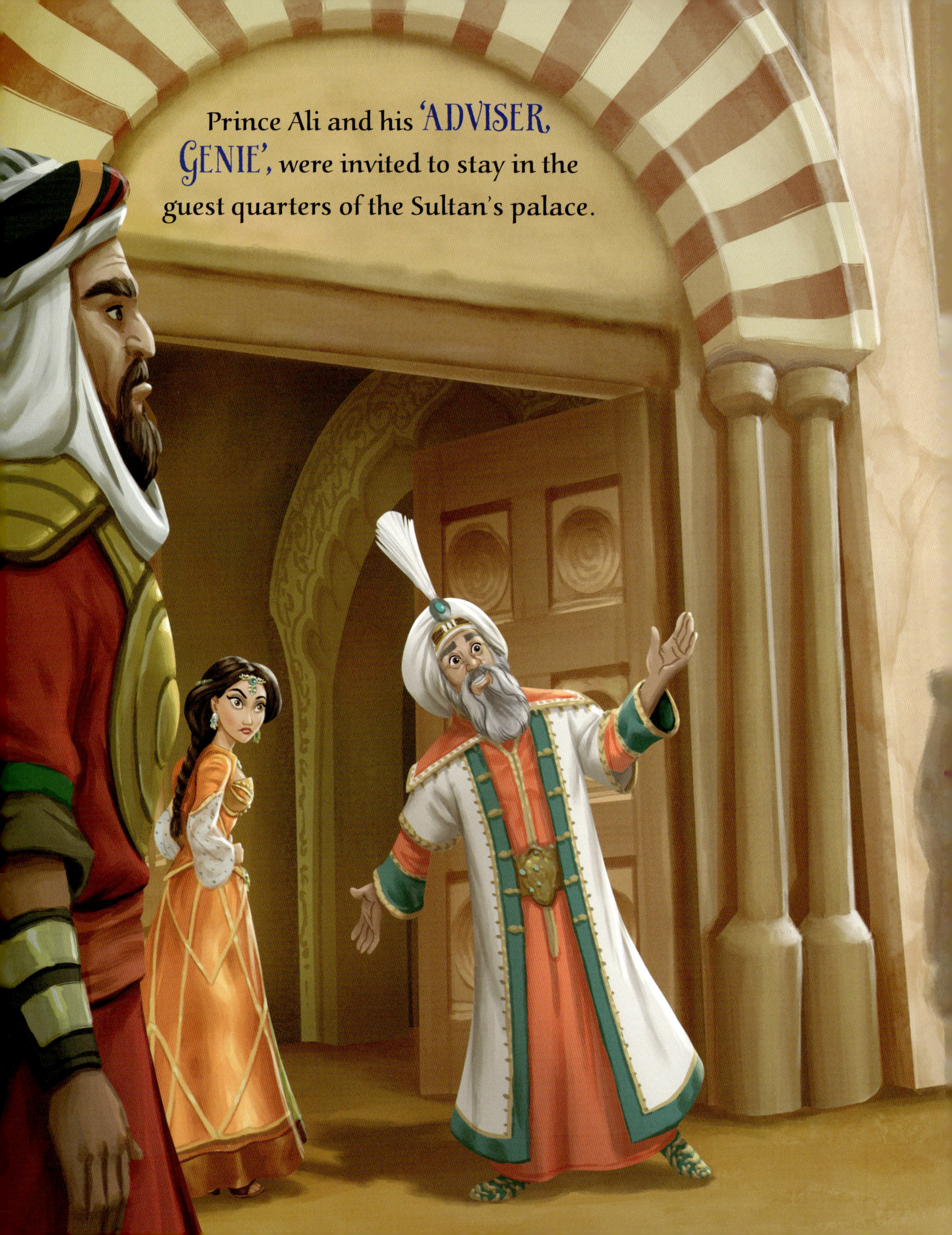
Prince Ali and his 'ADVISER, GENIE', were invited to stay in the guest quarters of the Sultan's palace.

Aladdin was nervous around Princess Jasmine, so Genie helped him work on his confidence.

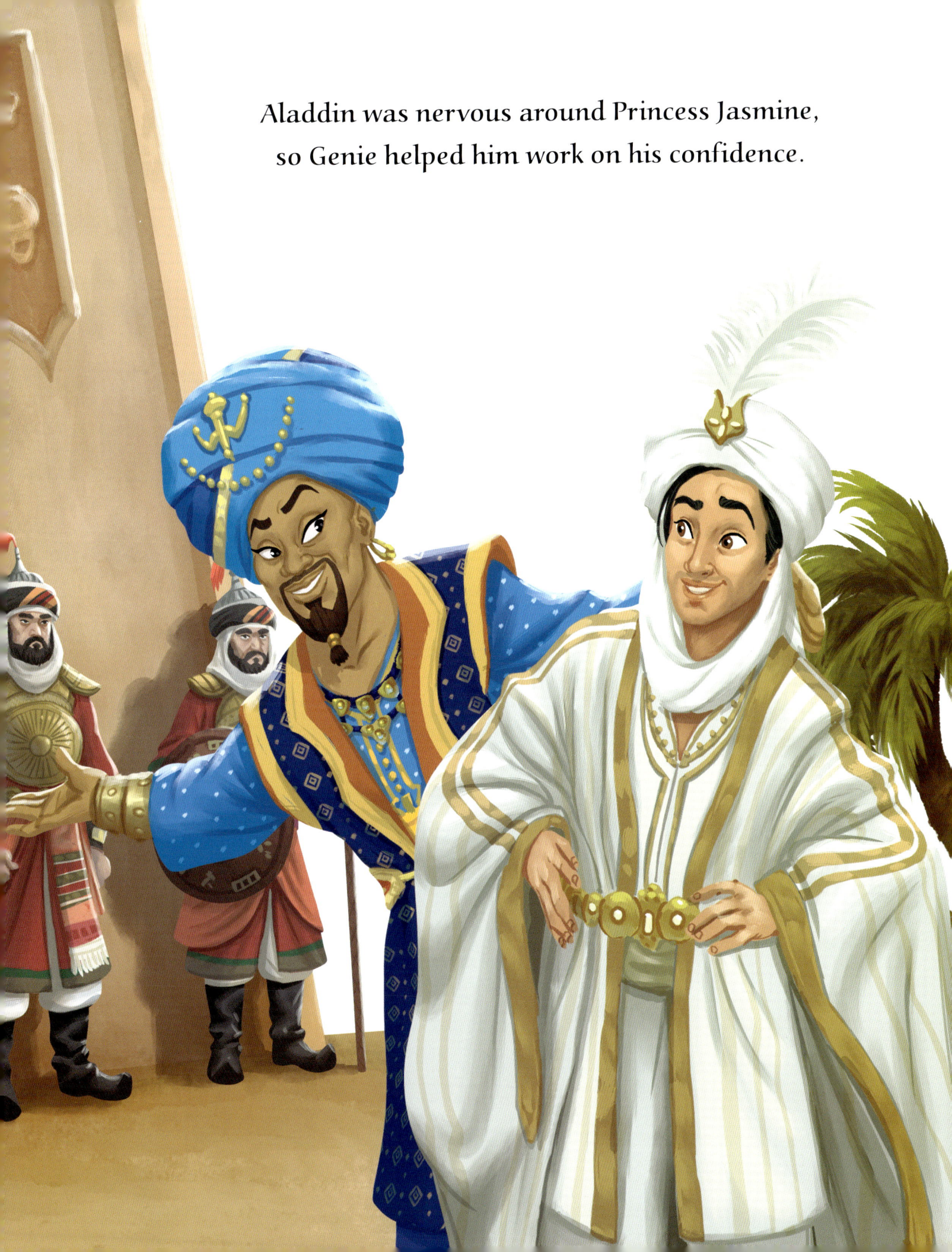

Genie and Aladdin spent a lot of time together, having fun and watching out for each other.

When Aladdin nearly drowned, Genie didn't hesitate to help him.

Aladdin was grateful to Genie for saving his life.
'THANK YOU, GENIE,' he said.

Genie was HAPPY that Aladdin was okay, and to his surprise, he realised... HE REALLY CARED ABOUT ALADDIN.

Aladdin surprised Genie again when he made his final wish. It wasn't for himself, but for

HIS GOOD FRIEND GENIE.

Aladdin and Genie both knew they had gotten something even a powerful genie couldn't grant:

A TRUE FRIEND.